Drowning With Others

Drowning With Others

POEMS BY *James Dickey*

WESLEYAN UNIVERSITY PRESS
Middletown, Connecticut

Among the poems in this volume are a number that have previously been printed elsewhere. Grateful acknowledgments are made to *The Atlantic Monthly, Choice, Encounter, Hudson Review, Kenyon Review, Partisan Review, Poetry, Poetry Dial, Quarterly Review of Literature, Sewanee Review, Virginia Quarterly Review,* and *Yale Review;* also to *The New Yorker,* in whose pages the following poems first appeared: "Autumn," "A Birth," "For the Nightly Ascent of the Hunter Orion Over a Forest Clearing," "The Heaven of Animals," "In the Mountain Tent," "In the Tree House at Night," "The Lifeguard," "Listening to Foxhounds," "The Magus," "The Movement of Fish," and "The Salt Marsh."

Library of Congress Catalog Card Number: 62–10570

Manufactured in the United States of America

First printing, February, 1962; second printing, November, 1963; third printing, November, 1965; fourth printing, October, 1966.

To Maxine, Christopher, and Kevin

Contents

Section I

The Lifeguard

In a stable of boats I lie still,
From all sleeping children hidden.
The leap of a fish from its shadow
Makes the whole lake instantly tremble.
With my foot on the water, I feel
The moon outside

Take on the utmost of its power.
I rise and go out through the boats.
I set my broad sole upon silver,
On the skin of the sky, on the moonlight,
Stepping outward from earth onto water
In quest of the miracle

This village of children believed
That I could perform as I dived
For one who had sunk from my sight.
I saw his cropped haircut go under.
I leapt, and my steep body flashed
Once, in the sun.

Dark drew all the light from my eyes.
Like a man who explores his death
By the pull of his slow-moving shoulders,
I hung head down in the cold,
Wide-eyed, contained, and alone
Among the weeds,

And my fingertips turned into stone
From clutching immovable blackness.
Time after time I leapt upward
Exploding in breath, and fell back
From the change in the children's faces
At my defeat.

Beneath them I swam to the boathouse
With only my life in my arms

11

To wait for the lake to shine back
At the risen moon with such power
That my steps on the light of the ripples
Might be sustained.

Beneath me is nothing but brightness
Like the ghost of a snowfield in summer.
As I move toward the center of the lake,
Which is also the center of the moon,
I am thinking of how I may be
The savior of one

Who has already died in my care.
The dark trees fade from around me.
The moon's dust hovers together.
I call softly out, and the child's
Voice answers through blinding water.
Patiently, slowly,

He rises, dilating to break
The surface of stone with his forehead.
He is one I do not remember
Having ever seen in his life.
The ground I stand on is trembling
Upon his smile.

I wash the black mud from my hands.
On a light given off by the grave
I kneel in the quick of the moon
At the heart of a distant forest
And hold in my arms a child
Of water, water, water.

Listening to Foxhounds

When in that gold
Of fires, quietly sitting
With the men whose brothers are hounds,

You hear the first tone
Of a dog on scent, you look from face
To face, to see whose will light up.

When that light comes
Inside the dark light of the fire,
You know which chosen man has heard

A thing like his own dead
Speak out in a marvelous, helpless voice
That he has been straining to hear.

Miles away in the dark,
His enchanted dog can sense
How his features glow like a savior's,

And begins to hunt
In a frenzy of desperate pride.
Among us, no one's eyes give off a light

For the red fox
Playing in and out of his scent,
Leaping stones, doubling back over water.

Who runs with the fox
Must sit here like his own image,
Giving nothing of himself

To the sensitive flames,
With no human joy rising up,
Coming out of his face to be seen.

And it is hard,

When the fox leaps into his burrow,
To keep that singing down,

To sit with the fire
Drawn into one's secret features,
And all eyes turning around

From the dark wood
Until they come, amazed, upon
A face that does not shine

Back from itself,
That holds its own light and takes more,
Like the face of the dead, sitting still,

Giving no sign,
Making no outcry, no matter
Who may be straining to hear.

A Dog Sleeping on my Feet

Being his resting place,
I do not even tense
The muscles of a leg
Or I would seem to be changing.
Instead, I turn the page
Of the notebook, carefully not

Remembering what I have written,
For now, with my feet beneath him
Dying like embers,
The poem is beginning to move
Up through my pine-prickling legs
Out of the night wood,

Taking hold of the pen by my fingers.
Before me the fox floats lightly,
On fire with his holy scent.
All, all are running.
Marvelous is the pursuit,
Like a dazzle of nails through the ankles,

Like a twisting shout through the trees
Sent after the flying fox
Through the holes of logs, over streams
Stock-still with the pressure of moonlight.
My killed legs,
My legs of a dead thing, follow,

Quick as pins, through the forest,
And all rushes on into dark
And ends on the brightness of paper.
When my hand, which speaks in a daze
The hypnotized language of beasts,
Shall falter, and fail

Back into the human tongue,
And the dog gets up and goes out

To wander the dawning yard,
I shall crawl to my human bed
And lie there smiling at sunrise,
With the scent of the fox

Burning my brain like an incense,
Floating out of the night wood,
Coming home to my wife and my sons
From the dream of an animal,
Assembling the self I must wake to,
Sleeping to grow back my legs.

The Movement of Fish

No water is still, on top.
Without wind, even, it is full
Of a chill, superficial agitation.
It is easy to forget,
Or not to know at all

That fish do not move
By means of this rippling
Along the outside of water, or
By anything touching on air.
Where they are, it is still,

Under a wooden bridge,
Under the poised oar
Of a boat, while the rower leans
And blows his mistaken breath
To make the surface shake,

Or yells at it, or sings,
Half believing the brilliant scan
Of ripples will carry the fish away
On his voice like a buried wind.
Or it may be that a fish

Is simply lying under
The ocean-broad sun
Which comes down onto him
Like a tremendous, suffusing
Open shadow

Of gold, where nothing is,
Sinking into the water,
Becoming dark around
His body. Where he is now
Could be gold mixed

With absolute blackness.

The surface at mid-sea shivers,
But he does not feel it
Like a breath, or like anything.
Yet suddenly his frame shakes,

Convulses the whole ocean
Under the trivial, quivering
Surface, and he is
Hundreds of feet away,
Still picking up speed, still shooting

Through half-gold,
Going nowhere. Nothing sees him.
One must think of this to understand
The instinct of fear and trembling,
And, of its one movement, the depth.

The Heaven of Animals

Here they are. The soft eyes open.
If they have lived in a wood
It is a wood.
If they have lived on plains
It is grass rolling
Under their feet forever.

Having no souls, they have come,
Anyway, beyond their knowing.
Their instincts wholly bloom
And they rise.
The soft eyes open.

To match them, the landscape flowers,
Outdoing, desperately
Outdoing what is required:
The richest wood,
The deepest field.

For some of these,
It could not be the place
It is, without blood.
These hunt, as they have done,
But with claws and teeth grown perfect,

More deadly than they can believe.
They stalk more silently,
And crouch on the limbs of trees,
And their descent
Upon the bright backs of their prey

May take years
In a sovereign floating of joy.
And those that are hunted
Know this as their life,
Their reward: to walk

Under such trees in full knowledge
Of what is in glory above them,
And to feel no fear,
But acceptance, compliance.
Fulfilling themselves without pain

At the cycle's center,
They tremble, they walk
Under the tree,
They fall, they are torn,
They rise, they walk again.

A Birth

Inventing a story with grass,
I find a young horse deep inside it.
I cannot nail wires around him;
My fence posts fail to be solid,

And he is free, strangely, without me.
With his head still browsing the greenness,
He walks slowly out of the pasture
To enter the sun of his story.

My mind freed of its own creature,
I find myself deep in my life
In a room with my child and my mother,
When I feel the sun climbing my shoulder

Change, to include a new horse.

Fog Envelops the Animals

Fog envelops the animals.
Not one can be seen, and they live.
At my knees, a cloud wears slowly
Up out of the buried earth.
In a white suit I stand waiting.

Soundlessly whiteness is eating
My visible self alive.
I shall enter this world like the dead,
Floating through tree trunks on currents
And streams of untouchable pureness

That shine without thinking of light.
My hands burn away at my sides
In the pale, risen ghosts of deep rivers.
In my hood peaked like a flame,
I feel my own long-hidden,

Long-sought invisibility
Come forth from my solid body.
I stand with all beasts in a cloud.
Of them I am deadly aware,
And they not of me, in this life.

Only my front teeth are showing
As the dry fog mounts to my lips
In a motion long buried in water,
And now, one by one, my teeth
Like rows of candles go out.

In the spirit of flame, my hood
Holds the face of my soul without burning,
And I drift forward
Through the hearts of the curdling oak trees,
Borne by the river of Heaven.

My arrows, keener than snowflakes,

Are with me whenever I touch them.
Above my head, the trees exchange their arms
In the purest fear upon earth.
Silence. Whiteness. Hunting.

The Summons

For something out of sight,
I cup a grass-blade in my hands,
Tasting the root, and blow.
I speak to the wind, and it lives.
No hunter has taught me this call;
It comes out of childhood and playgrounds.
I hang my longbow on a branch.
The wind at my feet extends

Quickly out, across the lake,
Containing the sound I have made.
The water below me becomes
Bright ploughland in its body.
I breathe on my thumbs, and am blowing
A horn that encircles the forest.
Across the lake, a tree
Now thrums in tremendous cadence.

Beneath it, some being stumbles,
And answers me slowly and greatly
With a tongue as rasping as sawgrass.
I lower my hands, and I listen
To the beast that shall die of its love.
I sound my green trumpet again,
And the whole wood sings in my palms.
The vast trees are tuned to my bowstring

And the deep-rooted voice I have summoned.
I have carried it here from a playground
Where I rolled in the grass with my brothers.
Nothing moves, but something intends to.
The water that puffed like a wing
Is one flattened blaze through the branches.
Something falls from the bank, and is swimming.
My voice turns around me like foliage,

And I pluck my longbow off the limb

Where it shines with a musical light,
And crouch within death, awaiting
The beast in the water, in love
With the palest and gentlest of children,
Whom the years have turned deadly with knowledge:
Who summons him forth, and now
Pulls wide the great, thoughtful arrow.

In the Tree House at Night

And now the green household is dark.
The half-moon completely is shining
On the earth-lighted tops of the trees.
To be dead, a house must be still.
The floor and the walls wave me slowly;
I am deep in them over my head.
The needles and pine cones about me

Are full of small birds at their roundest,
Their fists without mercy gripping
Hard down through the tree to the roots
To sing back at light when they feel it.
We lie here like angels in bodies,
My brothers and I, one dead,
The other asleep from much living,

In mid-air huddled beside me.
Dark climbed to us here as we climbed
Up the nails I have hammered all day
Through the sprained, comic rungs of the ladder
Of broom handles, crate slats, and laths
Foot by foot up the trunk to the branches
Where we came out at last over lakes

Of leaves, of fields disencumbered of earth
That move with the moves of the spirit.
Each nail that sustains us I set here;
Each nail in the house is now steadied
By my dead brother's huge, freckled hand.
Through the years, he has pointed his hammer
Up into these limbs, and told us

That we must ascend, and all lie here.
Step after step he has brought me,
Embracing the trunk as his body,
Shaking its limbs with my heartbeat,
Till the pine cones danced without wind

And fell from the branches like apples.
In the arm-slender forks of our dwelling

I breathe my live brother's light hair.
The blanket around us becomes
As solid as stone, and it sways.
With all my heart, I close
The blue, timeless eye of my mind.
Wind springs, as my dead brother smiles
And touches the tree at the root;

A shudder of joy runs up
The trunk; the needles tingle;
One bird uncontrollably cries.
The wind changes round, and I stir
Within another's life. Whose life?
Who is dead? Whose presence is living?
When may I fall strangely to earth,

Who am nailed to this branch by a spirit?
Can two bodies make up a third?
To sing, must I feel the world's light?
My green, graceful bones fill the air
With sleeping birds. Alone, alone
And with them I move gently.
I move at the heart of the world.

For the Nightly Ascent of the Hunter Orion Over a Forest Clearing

Now secretness dies of the open.
Yet all around, all over, night
Things are waking fast,
Waking with all their power.
Who can arise

From his dilating shadow
When one foot is longing to tiptoe
And the other to take the live
Stand of a tree that belongs here?
As the owl's gaze

Most slowly begins to create
Its sight from the death of the sun,
As the mouse feels the whole wood turn
The gold of the owl's new eyes,
And the fox moves

Out of the ground where he sleeps,
No man can stand upright
And drag his body forth
Through an open space in the foliage
Unless he rises

As does the hunter Orion,
Thinking to cross a blue hollow
Through the dangers of twilight,
Feeling that he must run
And that he will

Take root forever and stand,
Does both at once, and neither,
Grows blind, and then sees everything,
Steps and becomes a man
Of stars instead,

28

Who from invisibility
Has come, arranged in the light
Of himself, revealed tremendously
In his fabulous, rigid, eternal
Unlooked-for role.

The Rib

Something has left itself scattered
Under a bush in the evening,
Not recalling what lay down at first
To make its claimed body for years
Disappear into air,

Or lay with its small bones desiring
To come slowly forth into twilight
Where the moon begins to raise up
A dead tree now at my side.
I pick up a rib

And something like what must be
The bite small animals die of
Encircles myself and the tree,
Coming round again, coming closer,
A breath forming teeth,

Warming the bones of my wrist.
That my radiant palm is unopened,
That my breast is still whole
When I feel it seized on and thrown down
By the madness of hunting

Is a miracle, like the dead moon
Creating black trees with stone fire.
Can it be that the wounds of beasts,
The hurts they inherit no words for,
Are like the mouths

Of holy beings we think of,
So strongly do they breathe upon us
Their bloodletting silence?
A rib in my right side speaks
To me more softly

Than Eve—the bidden, unfreeable shape

Of my own unfinished desire
For life, for death and the Other—
So that the wound in the air
And its giver

Far off in the brush, all teeth,
Hear me answer the patient world
Of love in my side imprisoned
As I rise, going moonward toward better
And better sleep.

The Owl King

I

THE CALL

Through the trees, with the moon underfoot,
More soft than I can, I call.
I hear the king of the owls sing
Where he moves with my son in the gloom.
My tongue floats off in the darkness.
I feel the deep dead turn
My blind child round toward my calling,
Through the trees, with the moon underfoot,

In a sound I cannot remember.
It whispers like straw in my ear,
And shakes like a stone under water.
My bones stand on tiptoe inside it.
Which part of the sound did I utter?
Is it song, or is half of it whistling?
What spirit has swallowed my tongue?
Or is it a sound I remember?

And yet it is coming back,
Having gone, adrift on its spirit,
Down, over and under the river,
And stood in a ring in a meadow
Round a child with a bird gravely dancing.
I hear the king of the owls sing.
I did not awaken that sound,
And yet it is coming back,

In touching every tree upon the hill.
The breath falls out of my voice,
And yet the singing keeps on.
The owls are dancing, fastened by their toes
Upon the pines. Come, son, and find me here,
In love with the sound of my voice.

32

Come calling the same soft song,
And touching every tree upon the hill.

II

I swore to myself I would see
When all but my seeing had failed.
Every light was too feeble to show
My world as I knew it must be.
At the top of the staring night
I sat on the oak in my shape
With my claws growing deep into wood
And my sight going slowly out
Inch by inch, as into a stone,
Disclosing the rabbits running
Beneath my bent, growing throne,
And the foxes lighting their hair,
And the serpent taking the shape
Of the stream of life as it slept.
When I thought of the floating sound
In which my wings would outspread,
I felt the hooked tufts on my head
Enlarge, and dream like a crown,
And my voice unplaceable grow
Like a feathery sigh;
I could not place it myself.
For years I humped on the tree
Whose leaves held the sun and the moon.
At last I opened my eyes
In the sun, and saw nothing there.
That night I parted my lids
Once more, and saw dark burn
Greater than sunlight or moonlight,
For it burned from deep within me.
The still wood glowed like a brain.

I prised up my claws, and spread
My huge, ashen wings from my body,
For I heard what I listened to hear.
Someone spoke to me out of the distance
In a voice like my own, but softer.
I rose like the moon from the branch.

Through trees at his light touch trembling
The blind child drifted to meet me,
His blue eyes shining like mine.
In a ragged clearing he stopped,
And I circled, beating above him,
Then fell to the ground and hopped
Forward, taking his hand in my claw.
Every tree's life lived in his fingers.
Gravely we trod with each other
As beasts at their own wedding, dance.
Through the forest, the questioning voice
Of his father came to us there,
As though the one voice of us both,
Its high, frightened sound becoming
A perfect, irrelevant music
In which we profoundly moved,
I in the innermost shining
Of my blazing, invented eyes,
And he in the total of dark.
Each night, now, high on the oak,
With his father calling like music,
He sits with me here on the bough,
His eyes inch by inch going forward
Through stone dark, burning and picking
The creatures out one by one,
Each waiting alive in its own
Peculiar light to be found:
The mouse in its bundle of terror,
The fox in the flame of its hair,
And the snake in the form of all life.
Each night he returns to his bed,
To the voice of his singing father,

To dream of the owl king sitting
Alone in the crown of my will.
In my ruling passion, he rests.
All dark shall come to light.

III

THE BLIND CHILD'S STORY

I am playing going down
In my weight lightly,
Down, down the hill.
No one calls me
Out of the air.
The heat is falling
On the backs of my hands
And holding coldness.
They say it shines two ways.
The darkness is great
And luminous in my eyes.
Down I am quickly going;
A leaf falls on me,
It must be a leaf I hear it
Be thin against me, and now
The ground is level,
It moves it is not ground,
My feet flow cold
And wet, and water rushes
Past as I climb out.
I am there, on the other side.
I own the entire world.

It closes a little; the sky
Must be cold, must be giving off
Creatures that stand here.
I say they shine one way.

Trees they are trees around me,
Leaves branches and bark;
I can touch them all; I move
From one to another—someone said
I seem to be blessing them.
I am blessing them
Slowly, one after another
Deeper into the wood.

The dark is changing,
Its living is packed in closer
Overhead—more trees and leaves—
Tremendous. It touches
Something touches my hand,
Smelling it, a cold nose
Of breath, an ear of silk
Is gone. It is here I begin
To call to something unearthly.
Something is here, something before
Me sitting above me
In the wood in a crown,
Its eyes newborn in its head
From the death of the sun.
I can hear it rising on wings.
I hear that fluttering
Cease, and become
Pure soundless dancing
Like leaves not leaves;
Now down out of air
It lumbers to meet me,
Stepping oddly on earth,
Awkwardly, royally.
My father is calling

Through the touched trees;
All distance is weeping and singing.
In my hand I feel
A talon, a grandfather's claw
Bone cold and straining

To keep from breaking my skin.
I know this step, I know it,
And we are deep inside.
My father's voice is over
And under us, sighing.
Nothing is strange where we are.
The huge bird bows and returns,
For I, too, have done the same
As he leads me, rustling,
A pile of leaves in my hands;
The dry feathers shuffle like cards
On his dusty shoulders,
Not touching a tree,
Not brushing the side of a leaf
Or a point of grass.

We stop and stand like bushes.
But my father's music comes
In, goes on, comes in,
Into the wood,
Into the ceased dance.
And now the hard beak whispers
Softly, and we climb
Some steps of bark
Living and climbing with us
Into the leaves.
I sit among leaves,
And the whole branch hums
With the owl's full, weightless power
As he closes his feet on the wood.
My own feet dangle
And tingle down;
My head is pointing
Deep into moonlight,
Deep into branches and leaves,
Directing my blackness there,
The personal dark of my sight,
And now it is turning a color.
My eyes are blue at last.

Something within the place
I look is piled and coiled.
It lifts its head from itself.
Its form is lit, and gives back
What my eyes are giving it freely.
I learn from the master of sight
What to do when the sun is dead,
How to make the great darkness work
As it wants of itself to work.
I feel the tree where we sit
Grow under me, and live.
I may have been here for years;
In the coil, the heaped-up creature
May have taken that long to lift
His head, to break his tongue
From his thin lips,
But he is there. I shut my eyes
And my eyes are gold,
As gold as an owl's,
As gold as a king's.
I open them. Farther off,
Beyond the swaying serpent,
A creature is burning itself
In a smoke of hair through the bushes.
The fox moves; a small thing
Being caught, cries out,
And I understand
How beings and sounds go together;
I understand
The voice of my singing father.
I shall be king of the wood.

Our double throne shall grow
Forever, until I see
The self of every substance
As it crouches, hidden and free.
The owl's face runs with tears
As I take him in my arms
In the glow of original light

Of Heaven. I go down
In my weight lightly down
The tree, and now
Through the soul of the wood
I walk in consuming glory
Past the snake, the fox, and the mouse:
I see as the owl king sees,
By going in deeper than darkness.
The wood comes back in a light
It did not know it withheld,
And I can tell
By its breathing glow
Each tree on which I laid
My hands when I was blind.

I cross the cold-footed flowing,
The creek, a religious fire
Streaming my ankles away,
And climb through the slanted meadow.
My father cannot remember
That he ever lived in this house.
To himself he bays like a hound,
Entranced by the endless beauty
Of his grief-stricken singing and calling.
He is singing simply to moonlight,
Like a dog howling,
And it is holy song
Out of his mouth.
Father, I am coming,
I am here on my own;
I move as you sing,
As if it were Heaven.
It is Heaven. I am walking
To you and seeing
Where I walk home.
What I have touched, I see
With the dark of my blue eyes.
Far off, the owl king
Sings like my father, growing

In power. Father, I touch
Your face. I have not seen
My own, but it is yours.
I come, I advance,
I believe everything, I am here.

Section II

Between Two Prisoners

I would not wish to sit
In my shape bound together with wire,
Wedged into a child's sprained desk
In the schoolhouse under the palm tree.
Only those who did could have done it.

One bled from a cut on his temple,
And sat with his yellow head bowed,
His wound for him painfully thinking.
A belief in words grew upon them
That the unbound, who walk, cannot know.

The guard at the window leaned close
In a movement he took from the palm tree,
To hear, in a foreign tongue,
All things which cannot be said.
In the splintering clapboard room

They rested the sides of their faces
On the tops of the desks as they talked.
Because of the presence of children
In the deep signs carved in the desk tops,
Signs on the empty blackboard

Began, like a rain, to appear.
In the luminous chalks of all colors,
Green face, yellow breast, white sails
Whose wing feathers made the wall burn
Like a waterfall seen in a fever,

An angel came boldly to light
From his hands casting green, ragged bolts
Each having the shape of a palm leaf.
Also traced upon darkness in chalk
Was the guard at the rear window leaning

Through the red, vital strokes of his tears.

Behind him, men lying with swords
As with women, heard themselves sing,
And woke, then, terribly knowing
That they were a death squad, singing

In its sleep, in the middle of a war.
A wind sprang out of the tree.
The guard awoke by the window,
And found he had talked to himself
All night, in two voices, of Heaven.

He stood in the sunlit playground
Where the quiet boys knelt together
In their bloodletting trusses of wire,
And saw their mussed, severed heads
Make the ground jump up like a dog.

I watched the small guard be hanged
A year later, to the day,
In a closed horse stall in Manila.
No one knows what language he spoke
As his face changed into all colors,

And gave off his red, promised tears,
Or if he learned blindly to read
A child's deep, hacked hieroglyphics
Which can call up an angel from nothing,
Or what was said for an instant, there,

In the tied, scribbled dark, between him
And a figure drawn hugely in chalk,
Speaking words that can never be spoken
Except in a foreign tongue,
In the end, at the end of a war.

Armor

When this is the thing you put on
The world is pieced slowly together
In the power of the crab and the insect.
The make of the eyeball changes
As over your mouth you draw down
A bird's bill made for a man.

As your weight upon earth is redoubled
There is no way of standing alone
More, or no way of being
More with the bound, shining dead.
You have put on what you should wear,
Not into the rattling of battle,

But into a silence where nothing
Threatens but Place itself: the shade
Of the forest, the strange, crowned
Motionless sunlight of Heaven,
With the redbird blinking and shooting
Across the nailed beam of the eyepiece.

In that light, in the wood, in armor,
I look in myself for the being
I was in a life before life
In a glade more silent than breathing,
Where I took off my body of metal
Like a brother whose features I knew

By the feel of their strength on my face
And whose limbs by the shining of mine.
In a vision I fasten him there,
The bright locust shell of my strength
Like a hanged man waiting in Heaven,
And then steal off to my life.

In my home, a night nearer death,
I wake with no shield on my breastbone,

Breathing deep through my sides like an insect,
My closed hand falling and rising
Where it lies like the dead on my heart.
I cannot remember my brother;

Before I was born he went from me
Ablaze with the meaning of typhoid.
In a fever I see him turn slowly
Under the strange, perfect branches
Where somehow I left him to wait
That I might be naked on earth,

His crowned face dazzlingly closed,
His curving limbs giving off
Pure energy into the leaves.
When I give up my hold on my breath
I long to dress deeply at last
In the gold of my waiting brother

Who shall wake and shine on my limbs
As I walk, made whole, into Heaven.
I shall not remember his face
Or my dazed, eternal one
Until I have opened my hand
And touched the grave glow of his breast

To stop the gaunt turning of metal:
Until I have let the still sun
Down into the stare of the eyepiece
And raised its bird's beak to confront
What man is within to live with me
When I begin living forever.

In the Lupanar at Pompeii

There are tracks which belong to wheels
Long since turned to air and time.
Those are the powerful chariots
I follow down cobblestones,
Not being dragged, exactly,
But not of my own will, either,
Going past the flower sellers'
And the cindery produce market
And the rich man's home, and the house
Of the man who kept a dog
Set in mosaic.

As tourist, but mostly as lecher,
I seek out the dwelling of women
Who all expect me, still, because
They expect anybody who comes.
I am ready to pay, and I do,
And then go in among them
Where on the dark walls of their home
They hold their eternal postures,
Doing badly drawn, exacting,
Too-willing, wide-eyed things
With dry-eyed art.

I sit down in one of the rooms
Where it happened again and again.
I could be in prison, or dead,
Cast down for my sins in a cell
Still filled with a terrible motion
Like the heaving and sighing of earth
To be free of the heat it restrains.
I feel in my heart how the heart
Of the mountain broke, and the women
Fled onto the damp of the walls
And shaped their embraces

To include whoever would come here

After the stone-cutting chariots.
I think of the marvel of lust
Which can always, at any moment,
Become more than it believed,
And almost always is less:
I think of its possible passing
Beyond, into tender awareness,
Into helplessness, weeping, and death:
It must be like the first
Soft floating of ash,

When, in the world's frankest hands,
Someone lay with his body shaken
Free of the self: that amazement—
For we who must try to explain
Ourselves in the house of this flesh
Never can tell the quick heat
Of our own from another's breathing,
Nor yet from the floating of feathers
That form in our lungs when the mountain
Settles like odd, warm snow against
Our willing limbs.

We never can really tell
Whether nature condemns us or loves us
As we lie here dying of breath
And the painted, unchanging women,
Believing the desperate dead
Where they stripped to the skin of the soul
And whispered to us, as to
Their panting, observing selves:
"Passion. Before we die
Let us hope for no longer
But truly know it."

Drowning With Others

There are moments a man turns from us
Whom we have all known until now.
Upgathered, we watch him grow,
Unshipping his shoulder bones

Like human, everyday wings
That he has not ever used,
Releasing his hair from his brain,
A kingfisher's crest, confused

By the God-tilted light of Heaven.
His deep, window-watching smile
Comes closely upon us in waves,
And spreads, and now we are

At last within it, dancing.
Slowly we turn and shine
Upon what is holding us,
As under our feet he soars,

Struck dumb as the angel of Eden,
In wide, eye-opening rings.
Yet the hand on my shoulder fears
To feel my own wingblades spring,

To feel me sink slowly away
In my hair turned loose like a thought
Of a fisherbird dying in flight.
If I opened my arms, I could hear

Every shell in the sea find the word
It has tried to put into my mouth.
Broad flight would become of my dancing,
And I would obsess the whole sea,

But I keep rising and singing
With my last breath. Upon my back,

With his hand on my unborn wing,
A man rests easy as sunlight

Who has kept himself free of the forms
Of the deaf, down-soaring dead,
And me laid out and alive
For nothing at all, in his arms.

A View of Fujiyama After the War

Wind, and all the midges in the air,
On wings you cannot see, awake
Where they must have been sleeping in flight.
I breathe, and twenty mile away

Snow streams from the mountain top
And all other mountains are nothing.
The ground of the enemy's country
Shakes; my bones settle back where they stand.

Through the bloom of gnats in the sun,
Shaken less than my heart by the tremor,
The blossom of a cherry tree appears.
The mountain returns my last breath,

And my hair blows, weightless as snow.
When it is still, when it is as still as this,
It could be a country where no one
Ever has died but of love.

I take the snow's breath and I speak it.
What I say has the form of a flame
Going all through the gnats like their spirit,
And for a swarming moment they become,

Almost, my own drunk face in the air
Against the one mountain in Heaven.
It is better to wait here quietly,
Not for my face to take flight,

But for someone to come from the dead
Other side of the war to this place:
Who thinks of this ground as his home,
Who thinks no one else can be here,

And that no one can see him pass
His hand through a visage of insects,

His hand through the cone of the mountain
To pluck the flower. But will he feel

His sobbing be dug like a wellspring
Or a deep water grow from his lids
To light, and break up the mountain
Which sends his last breath from its summit

As it dances together again?
Can he know that to live at the heart
Of his saved, shaken life, is to stand
Overcome by the enemy's peace?

The Island

A light come from my head
Showed how to give birth to the dead
That they might nourish me.
In a wink of the blinding sea
I woke through the eyes, and beheld
No change, but what had been,
And what cannot be seen
Any place but a burnt-out war:
The engines, the wheels, and the gear
That bring good men to their backs
Nailed down into wooden blocks,
With the sun on their faces through sand,
And polyps a-building the land
Around them of senseless stone.
The coral and I understood
That these could come to no good
Without the care I could give,
And that I, by them, must live.
I clasped every thought in my head
That bloomed from the magical dead,
And seizing a shovel and rake,
Went out by the ocean to take
My own sweet time, and start
To set a dead army apart.
I hammered the coffins together
Of patience and hobnails and lumber,
And gave them names, and hacked
Deep holes where they were stacked.
Each wooden body, I took
In my arms, and singingly shook
With its being, which stood for my own
More and more, as I laid it down.
At the grave's crude, dazzling verge
My true self strained to emerge
From all they could not save
And did not know they could give.
I buried them where they lay

In the brass-bound heat of the day,
A whole army lying down
In animal-lifted sand.
And then with rake and spade
I curried each place I had stood
On their chests and on their faces,
And planted the rows of crosses
Inside the blue wind of the shore.
I hauled more wood to that ground
And a white fence put around
The soldiers lying in waves
In my life-giving graves.
And a painless joy came to me
When the troopships took to the sea,
And left the changed stone free
Of all but my image and me:
Of the tonsured and perilous green
With its great, delighted design
Of utter finality,
Whose glowing workman stood
In the intricate, knee-high wood
In the midst of the sea's blind leagues,
Kicked off his old fatigues,
Saluted the graves by their rank,
Paraded, lamented, and sank
Into the intelligent light,
And danced, unimagined and free,
Like the sun taking place on the sea.

Section III

Dover: Believing in Kings

As we drove down the ramp from the boat
The sun flashed once
Or through hand-shieldedly twice;
In a silence out of a sound
We watched for channel swimmers dim with grease,
Come, here, to the ale of the shallows.
Within a wind, a wind sprang slowly up.
Birds hovered where they were.
As they were there, the airstream of the cliffs
Overcame, came over them
In the sackcloth and breast-beating gray
The king wears newly, at evening.
In a movement you cannot imagine
Of air, the gulls fall, shaken.

No stronger than the teeth in my head
Or a word laid bare
On chilling glass, the breathed stone over us rode.
From its top, the eye may sail,
Outgrowing the graven nerves
Of the brow's long-thought-out lines,
To France, on its own color.
From a child's tall book, I knew this place
The child must believe, with the king:
Where, doubtless, now, lay lovers
Restrained by a cloud, and the moon
Into force coming justly, above.
In a movement you cannot imagine
Of love, the gulls fall, mating.

We stopped; the birds hung up their arms
Inside the wind
So that they heeled; above, around us,
Their harp-strung feathers made
The sound, quickly mortal, of sighing.
We watched them in pure obsession.
Where they did move, we moved

Along the cliffs, the promenade,
The walls, the pebble beach,
And felt the inmost island turn,
In their cross-cut, wing-walking cries,
To a thing, as weeping, sensitive,
And haunted by the balancement of light
The king wears newly, in singing.

We wandered off from the car
In the light, half-sun,
Half-moon, in a worn-down shine out of stone,
And the taste of an iron ladle on the wind.
In the moon's grimed, thumbprint silver
The anchor spoke through the bell,
Far out, the hour that hung in the sea.
I threw a slow-flying stone; it dropped
Inside the brilliant echo of a light.
In a great, clustered, overdrawn sigh
The gulls went up, on a raiment of wings
The king wears newly, in panic.
In a movement you cannot imagine
Of error, the gulls rise, wholly.

We climbed a wall they had flown.
Each light below
On water, quivered like a thing in a lathe.
In the heron crest of a lamp,
Among lights, in their treading motion,
The head of my reflection seemed to sing
A dark, quickened side of the truth.
I touched my wife. I saw my son, unborn,
Left living after me, and my Self,
There, freed of myself,
In a stricken shade dancing together,
As a wave rolled under the water,
Lifted and rose in our images
The king wears newly, redoubling.

Where we went in, all power failed the house.

I spooned out light
Upon a candle thread. My wife lay down.
Through the flaming, white-bread nerve
I peered from the eye of the mind.
No child from the windowed dark came forth
To the hand, in its pure-blooded fire,
But the basket glow of the crown.
The glass fetched white to a breath; I understood
How the crown must come from within:
Of water made, and a wheel,
And of the thing in flame that seems to pant.
In a movement you cannot imagine
Of mirrors, the gulls fall, hidden.

I lay in bed. One hand in its sleeve
Lay open, on my breath.
My shadow dancing stilly beneath me
Rose, through my form. I heard the bell,
In mist, step backwardly onto the waves.
The wind fell off, as candle shade
Unraveled our walls like knitting, and I,
Undone, outstretched through the trampled shining
Of thousands of miles of the moon,
And the fallen king
Breathed like a nosebleed, there,
Two men wear newly, in hiding.
In a movement you cannot imagine
Of bloodshed, the gulls fall, inward.

I listened for the coming of a barge.
In a cat's-cradling motion
Of oars, my father rocked, in the mist. He died;
He was dying. His whisper fell,
As I, beneath the grave. Below the drowned
I panted, in the pig-iron taste of my beard.
I yelled, as out of a bucket,
Through my fettered mask, before the dawn
When my arms, my big-footed legs would hang
From pothooks, strange and untimely.

59

The stone beat like a gull; my father's voice
Came to life, in words, in my ear.
In a movement you cannot imagine
Of prison, the gulls turn, calling.

Believing, then, astoundedly, in a son,
I drew from tufted stone
My sword. I slew my murderer, Lightborn, on the stair:
With the flat of steel, I flashed
Him dead, through his eyes high-piled in the hood.
When the tide came in, I rose
And onto the curded dark climbed out.
In the cliffs, where creatures about me swam,
In their thin, slain, time-serving bones,
The heavy page, the animal print of the chalk,
With wounds I glittered, dazzling as a fish.
In my short-horned, wool-gathering crown
I came from the beasts to the kingdoms
The king wears newly, in passing.

The sun fell down, through the moon.
The dead held house.
I hove my father to my back
And climbed from his barrow, there.
Pride helped me pick a queen and get a son.
The heroic drink of the womb
Broke, then, into swanlike song.
One came with scepter, one with cup,
One goatlike back'd, and one with the head of a god.
My mask fell away, and my gyves.
Through my sons I leapt in my ghost
The king wears newly, on fire.
In a movement you cannot imagine
Of birth, the gulls fall, crying.

In the cloudlike, packed, and layered realm
I wept, when I would sing.
I laid my father down where he must lie,

And entered, again, in my passion,
An older, incredible shape
Becoming young, as the cliffs let fall within stone
Their shadow green down from the crest.
I stood on the cliff top, alone.
My father's body in my heart
Like a buried candle danced. I saw it shed on the sea,
On the flats of water, far out:
A rough, selected brightness
Exchanging a flame for a wheel
The king wears slowly, in measure.

Birds drifted in my breath as it was drawn
From the stressing glitter
Of water. Where France becomes
Another blue lid for the eye,
I felt my green eyes turn
Surpassingly blue, of one great look upon distance.
The sword dissolved, in my hands; wings beat.
I watched them rise from my arms, and stood
Excited forever by love. I saw the child's eye shine
From his book, a wave of justified light.
The prisons like organs moaned. In a death like life
I sang like a head on a pole.
In a movement you cannot imagine
Of emblems, the gulls fall, silent.

One foot shone to me, from the sun.
I felt the sun's
Mortality increase. In the blown,
Brow-beating light, I woke, and saw the room
Arise like a yeast from the floor,
The window come down like a bee.
In the long-legged, warm-bodied bed
I thought of him who would tell
To himself, arising in his candle-cast bones:
Every man, every man
Not a king. It is I

The king wears newly, in lasting.
In a movement you cannot imagine
Of spells, the gulls fall, listening.

How shall the stranger wake
Who has issued from dark
With the king? With gulls asleep
In the blue-burning grass? And on the sea,
A blaze that is counting itself,
The white birds holding
Still, on the field of the cloth of gold,
On the self and soul of the air?
Who stands, big-footed with glory, yet,
With the sound falling out of his voice
And his voice halfway to his son
Whose breath Time holds, in a woman?
In a movement you cannot imagine
Of silence, the gulls fall, waiting.

Why not as a prince, who, as
From a distance, wakes?
Who turns from the regular mirror
To watch, at the flawing pane,
Pale fire on a hairspring still burning
In the puddled socket, and the fishing flash
On the shuffled rock of a wave
Overturn, in an inlaid crash
In the window's half-mirror, half-air
As he steps through this room from the sea?
A tossed, green crown on his head,
He combs down the hair of his spirit,
Which is dead, but for the eyes
The king wears newly, at thirty:

Yet who is *he?* Whom does he face, in reflection?
The stained-glass king,
Or the child, grown tall, who cried to earth and air,
To books and water: to sun and father and fire
And nothingness to come and crown him, here?

Or are they, both of them, and neither,
This straw-headed knave, in blue-printed blue jeans appear-
ing:
Who, in exultant tenderness upon a woman's sleep
Onlooks, then leaps out the door, out of that
Up onto the seaside path, and when the sheep track dies,
Two late and idle lovers in the grass
Kicks into love, and goes up the cliffs to be crowned?
In a movement you cannot imagine
Of England, the king smiles, climbing: running.

To His Children in Darkness

You hear my step
Come close, and stop.
I shut the door.
By the two-deck bed
And its breathing sheets
Houselight is killed
From off my breast.
I am unseen,
But sensed, but known,
And now begin

To be what I
Can never be,
But what I am
Within your dream:
A god or beast
Come true at last.
To one, I have
Like leaves grown here,
And furl my wings
As poplars sigh,

And slowly let
On him a breath
Drawn in a cloud,
In which he sees
Angelic hosts
Like blowing trees
Send me to earth
To root among
The secret soil
Of his dark room.

The other hears
A creature shed
Throughout the maze
The same long breath

As he conceives
That he no more
Desires to live
In blazing sun,
Nor shake to death
The animal

Of his own head.
I know what lies
Behind all words,
Like a beast, mismade,
Which finds its brain
Can sing alone
Without a sound
At what he is
And cannot change,
Or like a god

Which slowly breathes
Eternal life
Upon a soul
In deepest sleep.
My heart's one move
Comes now, and now.
A god strikes root
On touching earth.
A beast can hold
The thought of self

Between his horns
Until it shines.
That you may feel
What I must be
And cannot know
By standing here,
My sons, I bring
These beings home
Into your room.
They are. I am.

A Screened Porch in the Country

All of them are sitting
Inside a lamp of coarse wire
And being in all directions
Shed upon darkness,
Their bodies softening to shadow, until
They come to rest out in the yard
In a kind of blurred golden country
In which they more deeply lie
Than if they were being created
Of Heavenly light.

Where they are floating beyond
Themselves, in peace,
Where they have laid down
Their souls and not known it,
The smallest creatures,
As every night they do,
Come to the edge of them
And sing, if they can,
Or, if they can't, simply shine
Their eyes back, sitting on haunches,

Pulsating and thinking of music.
Occasionally, something weightless
Touches the screen
With its body, dies,
Or is unmurmuringly hurt,
But mainly nothing happens
Except that a family continues
To be laid down
In the midst of its nightly creatures,
Not one of which openly comes

Into the golden shadow
Where the people are lying,
Emitted by their own house
So humanly that they become

More than human, and enter the place
Of small, blindly singing things,
Seeming to rejoice
Perpetually, without effort,
Without knowing why
Or how they do it.

The Dream Flood

I ask and receive
The secret of falling unharmed
Forty nights from the darkness of Heaven,
Coming down in sheets and in atoms
Until I descend to the moon

Where it lies on the ground
And finds in my surface the shining
It knew it must have in the end.
No longer increasing, I stand
Taking sunlight transmitted by stone,

And then begin over fields
To expand like a mind seeking truth,
Piling fathoms of brightness in valleys,
Letting no hilltop break through me.
As I rise, the moon rises also

As the reborn look of creation
In the animals' eyes,
In the eyes of horses in stables
Who feel their warm heaviness swarm
Out of their mouths like their souls;

Their bodies in cell blocks of wood
Hang like a dust that has taken
Their shapes without knowing of horses.
When the straight sun strikes them at last
Their grains congeal as they must

And nail their scuffed hoofs to the earth.
I withdraw, in feeling the cloud
Of Heaven call dazzlingly to me
To drop off my horses and forests,
To leave a vague mist in the valleys

And the hilltops steaming.

O grasses and fence wire of glory
That have burned like a coral with depth,
Understand that I have stood shining
About loved and abandoned women:

For acres around their thin beds
Which lifted like mesmerized tables
And danced in mid-air of their rooms
Like the chairs that children dance with,
So that each, hanging deep in her morning

Rose-colored bath, shall implore
Those impotent waters, and sunlight
Straining in vain
With her lost, dead weight:
"Lift. I am dreaming. Lift."

The Scratch

Once hid in a fiery twist
Of brier, it binds my wrist.
In this marked place, on a stone,
I watchfully sit down
To lift it wisely, and see
Blood come, as at a play,
Which shall fall outside my life.
It knows neither stone nor leaf,
Nor how it has come from my heart
To find its true color in light.
The glaze of my death is upon it
In the shadowy sun, and yet
A merciful rust shall set in
To kill, not me, but my pain.
My arm opened up by a thorn,
I feel the no-soul of the rock;
I hear, through the trees, the cock
Shout out his long-necked cry.
My patience comes over the wood,
And, caught in the silence of blood,
The wind in the leaves stands still
And delivers its green to my will.
I raise my other-armed sleeve,
And wipe, in a kind of love,
The wellspring of love from its bed,
And, glancing about for the dead,
Look distantly off at my blood
As it forms upon air, as if
It were the first blood of my life,
And the last thing of earth that I owned.
I conjure up sons, all crowned,
Who this drop shall not inherit,
And women who shall not share it,
Who might have borne me that son
To sit on a moss-backed stone
And master the kingdom of silence
Forever: as I do, once.

I feel more alive thereby
Than when the same blood in my eye
Of sleep, brought my real son,
Or my wife, that heavenly one.
I have had no vision but this
Of blood unable to pass
Between father and son,
Yet wedding the brain and the stone,
The cock's cutting cry and the thorn,
And binding me, whole, in a wood,
To a prince of impossible blood.
The rock shall inherit my soul.
The gem at my wrist is dull,
And may or may never fall.
Which will be, I do not know.
I shall dream of a crown till I do.

Hunting Civil War Relics at
Nimblewill Creek

As he moves the mine detector
A few inches over the ground,
Making it vitally float
Among the ferns and weeds,
I come into this war
Slowly, with my one brother,
Watching his face grow deep
Between the earphones,
For I can tell
If we enter the buried battle
Of Nimblewill
Only by his expression.

Softly he wanders, parting
The grass with a dreaming hand.
No dead cry yet takes root
In his clapped ears
Or can be seen in his smile.
But underfoot I feel
The dead regroup,
The burst metals all in place,
The battle lines be drawn
Anew to include us
In Nimblewill,
And I carry the shovel and pick

More as if they were
Bright weapons that I bore.
A bird's cry breaks
In two, and into three parts.
We cross the creek; the cry
Shifts into another,
Nearer, bird, and is
Like the shout of a shadow—
Lived-with, appallingly close—
Or the soul, pronouncing

"Nimblewill":
Three tones; your being changes.

We climb the bank;
A faint light glows
On my brother's mouth.
I listen, as two birds fight
For a single voice, but he
Must be hearing the grave,
In pieces, all singing
To his clamped head,
For he smiles as if
He rose from the dead within
Green Nimblewill
And stood in his grandson's shape.

No shot from the buried war
Shall kill me now,
For the dead have waited here
A hundred years to create
Only the look on the face
Of my one brother,
Who stands among them, offering
A metal dish
Afloat in the trembling weeds,
With a long-buried light on his lips
At Nimblewill
And the dead outsinging two birds.

I choke the handle
Of the pick, and fall to my knees
To dig wherever he points,
To bring up mess tin or bullet,
To go underground
Still singing, myself,
Without a sound,
Like a man who renounces war,
Or one who shall lift up the past,
Not breathing "Father,"
At Nimblewill,
But saying, "Fathers! Fathers!"

The Twin Falls

They fall through my life and surround me
Where I stand on a stone held between them,
And help them sing down the lifting

Of leaves in the springtime valley.
If I move my bare arms, the wings
Of water shake and are whiter.

I dance on the unshaken stone
And the rock rises up in my voice
As water the shape of my shoulders

Falls past without passing or moving.
Lifting up the blind spirit of bedrock,
My voice falls in waves on the green

Held up in a storm to receive it,
Where trees with their roots in my standing
Are singing it back to surround me

And telling me how my light body
Falls through the still years of my life
On great, other wings than its own.

The Hospital Window

I have just come down from my father.
Higher and higher he lies
Above me in a blue light
Shed by a tinted window.
I drop through six white floors
And then step out onto pavement.

Still feeling my father ascend,
I start to cross the firm street,
My shoulder blades shining with all
The glass the huge building can raise.
Now I must turn round and face it,
And know his one pane from the others.

Each window possesses the sun
As though it burned there on a wick.
I wave, like a man catching fire.
All the deep-dyed windowpanes flash,
And, behind them, all the white rooms
They turn to the color of Heaven.

Ceremoniously, gravely, and weakly,
Dozens of pale hands are waving
Back, from inside their flames.
Yet one pure pane among these
Is the bright, erased blankness of nothing.
I know that my father is there,

In the shape of his death still living.
The traffic increases around me
Like a madness called down on my head.
The horns blast at me like shotguns,
And drivers lean out, driven crazy—
But now my propped-up father

Lifts his arm out of stillness at last.
The light from the window strikes me

And I turn as blue as a soul,
As the moment when I was born.
I am not afraid for my father—
Look! He is grinning; he is not

Afraid for my life, either,
As the wild engines stand at my knees
Shredding their gears and roaring,
And I hold each car in its place
For miles, inciting its horn
To blow down the walls of the world

That the dying may float without fear
In the bold blue gaze of my father.
Slowly I move to the sidewalk
With my pin-tingling hand half dead
At the end of my bloodless arm.
I carry it off in amazement,

High, still higher, still waving,
My recognized face fully mortal,
Yet not; not at all, in the pale,
Drained, otherworldly, stricken,
Created hue of stained glass.
I have just come down from my father.

Section IV

The Magus

It is time for the others to come.
This child is no more than a god.

No cars are moving this night.
The lights in the houses go out.

I put these out with the rest.
From his crib, the child begins

To shine, letting forth one ray
Through the twelve simple bars of his bed

Down into the trees, where two
Long-lost other men shall be drawn

Slowly up to the brink of the house,
Slowly in through the breath on the window.

But how did I get in this room?
Is this my son, or another's?

Where is the woman to tell me
How my face is lit up by his body?

It is time for the others to come.
An event more miraculous yet

Is the thing I am shining to tell you.
This child is no more than a child.

Antipolis

Through the town-making stones I step lightly.
Each thing in the market place looks
Clear through me, not able to help it.
Squid lounging in death in their barrel
See me staring through life down among them.
They deepen the depth of their gaze.
The eyes of the dead hold me brightly.
I take all their looks into mine
And lift them up

Alive, and carry them out through the door
The Greeks made to give on the sea.
The world opens wide and turns blue.
My heart shines in me like sunlight.
I scramble up sill after sill,
Past windows where women are washing
My strange, heavy, foreigner's clothes.
My voice in amazement dwindles
To that of a child,

And with it I call to my son,
Who reads Greek somewhere below me.
He answers; a dead tongue sings.
I leap to the bread-colored rampart,
And stroll there, sweating and staring
Down into the powder-blue ocean
With dozens of dead, round, all-seeing eyes
In my head, which have seen ships sink
Through this water

And gods rise, wearing their sails.
A hundred feet over the ocean,
My hands dead white with the flour
Of the market, knowing and saying
The same timeless thought as the sun,
Which thinks of itself in its glory
As Pericles' head on a coin,

I hear in my voice two children,
My son and my soul,

Sing to each other through ages.
In the windows, men with their women
Among my dark garments burn cleanly.
Because I am drunk on the rampart,
My son reads Homer more deeply,
And the blue sea has caught me alive
In my own glance, the look of some daring,
Unbelieved, believing and dancing
Most loving creature.

The Change

Blue, unstirrable, dreaming,
The hammerhead goes by the boat,
Passing me slowly in looking.

He has singled me out from the others;
He has put his blue gaze in my brain.
The strength of creation sees through me:

The world is yet blind as beginning.
The shark's brutal form never changes.
No millions of years shall yet turn him

From himself to a man in love,
Yet I feel that impossible man
Hover near, emerging from darkness,

Like a creature of light from the ocean.
He is what I would make of myself
In ten million years, if I could,

And arise from my brute of a body
To a thing the world never thought of
In a place as apparent as Heaven.

I name the blue shark in the water,
And the heart of my brain has spoken
To me, like an unknown brother,

Gently of ends and beginnings,
Gently of sources and outcomes,
Impossible, brighter than sunlight.

Autumn

I see the tree think it will turn
Brown, and tomorrow at dawn
It will change as it thinks it will change,

But faster, bringing in orange,
And smoking and king-killing gold.
The fire of death shall change colors,

But before its rich images die,
Some green will be thought of in glory.
The dead shall withhold it until

The sleep of the world take on
The air of awaiting an angel
To descend into Hell, and to blow

With his once-a-year breath upon grass roots,
And deliver the year from its thinking
To the mindless one color of life.

Snow on a Southern State

Alongside the train I labor
To change wholly into my spirit,
As the place of my birth falls upward

Into the snow,
And my pale, sealed face looks in
From the world where it ripples and sails,
Sliding through culverts,

Plunging through tunnels while flakes
Await my long, streaming return
As they wait for this country to rise

And become something else in mid-air.
With a just-opened clicking, I come
Forth into fresh, buried meadows
Of muffled night light

Where people still sit on their porches
Screened in for eternal summer,
Watching the snow

Like grated shadow sift
Impossibly to them.
Through the window I tell them dumbly
That the snow is like

A man, stretched out upon landscape
And a spotless berth,
Who is only passing through

Their country, who means no harm:
Who stares in distrust at his ghost
Also flying, feet first, through the distance.
Numbly, the lips of his spirit

Move, and a fur-bearing steeple looms up

Through the heart of his mirrored breast.
The small town where he was born

Assembles around it,
The neon trying, but obviously unreal,
The parked cars clumsily letting
Pureness, a blinding burden,

Come slowly upon them.
All are still, all are still,
For the breath-holding window and I

Only must move through the silence,
Bearing my huge, prone ghost
Up, out, and now flying over
The vapor-lamp-glowing high school

Into the coming fields
Like a thing we cannot put down.
Yet the glass gives out of my image

And the laid clicking dies, as the land
All around me shines with the power
Of renewing my youth
By changing the place where I lived it.

There is nothing here, now, to watch
The bedclothes whirl into flakes.
What should be warm in these blankets

Has powdered down into its own
Steel-blue and feathery visions
Of weddings opposed by the world:
Is hovering over

A dead cotton field, which awaits
Its touch as awaiting completion:
Is building the pinewoods again

85

For this one night of their lives:
With the equilibrium
Of bones, is falling, falling,
Falling into the river.

To Landrum Guy, Beginning to Write at Sixty

One man in a house
Consumed by the effort of listening,
Sets down a worried phrase upon a paper.
It is poor, though it has come

From the table as out of a wall,
From his hand as out of his heart.

To sixty years it has come
At the same rate of time as he.
He cannot tell it, ever, what he thinks.
It is time, he says, he must

Be thinking of nothing but singing,
Be singing of nothing but love.

But the right word cannot arrive
Through the dark, light house of one man
With his savage hand on a book,
With a cricket seizing slowly on his ear:

One man in a house cannot hear
His ear, with his hair falling out from the quick.

Even to himself he cannot say
Except with not one word,
How he hears there is no more light
Than this, nor any word

More anywhere: how he is drunk
On hope, and why he calls himself mad.

Weeping is steadily built, and does not fall
From the shadow sitting slowly behind him
On the wall, like an angel who writes him a letter
To tell him his only talent is too late

To tell, to weep, to speak, or to begin
Here, or ever. Here, where he begins.

Facing Africa

These are stone jetties,
And, in the close part of the night,
Connected to my feet by long
Warm, dangling shadows
On the buttressed water,
Boats are at rest.

Beyond, the harbor mouth opens
Much as you might believe
A human mouth would open
To say that all things are a darkness.
I sit believing this
As the boats beneath me dissolve

And shake with a haunted effort
To come into being again,
And my son nods at my side,
Looking out also
Into dark, through the painted
Living shadows of dead-still hulls

Toward where we imagine Africa
To bloom late at night
Like a lamp of sand held up,
A top-heavy hourglass, perhaps,
With its heaped, eternal grains
Falling, falling

Into the lower, green part
Which gives off quick, leafy flashes
Like glimpses of lightning.
We strain to encounter that image
Halfway from its shore to ours:
To understand

The undermined glowing of sand
Lifted at midnight

Somewhere far out above water,
The effortless flicker of trees
Where a rumor of beasts moves slowly
Like wave upon wave.

What life have we entered by this?
Here, where our bodies are,
With a green and gold light on his face,
My staring child's hand is in mine,
And in the stone
Fear like a dancing of peoples.

Inside the River

Dark, deeply. A red.
All levels moving
A given surface.
Break this. Step down.
Follow your right
Foot nakedly in
To another body.
Put on the river
Like a fleeing coat,
A garment of motion,
Tremendous, immortal.
Find a still root

To hold you in it.
Let flowing create
A new, inner being:
As the source in the mountain
Gives water in pulses,
These can be felt at
The heart of the current.
And here it is only
One wandering step
Forth, to the sea.
Your freed hair floating
Out of your brain,

Wait for a coming
And swimming idea.
Live like the dead
In their flying feeling.
Loom as a ghost
When life pours through it.
Crouch in the secret
Released underground
With the earth of the fields
All around you, gone
Into purposeful grains

That stream like dust

In a holy hallway.
Weight more changed
Than that of one
Now being born,
Let go the root.
Move with the world
As the deep dead move,
Opposed to nothing.
Release. Enter the sea
Like a winding wind.
No. Rise. Draw breath.
Sing. See no one.

The Salt Marsh

Once you have let the first blade
Spring back behind you
To the way it has always been,
You no longer know where you are.
All you can see are the tall
Stalks of sawgrass, not sawing,
But each of them holding its tip
Exactly at the level where your hair

Begins to grow from your forehead.
Wherever you come to is
The same as before,
With the same blades of oversized grass,
And wherever you stop, the one
Blade just in front of you leans,
That one only, and touches you
At the place where your hair begins

To grow; at that predestined touch
Your spine tingles crystally, like salt,
And the image of a crane occurs,
Each flap of its wings creating
Its feathers anew, this time whiter,
As the sun destroys all points
Of the compass, refusing to move
From its chosen noon.

Where is the place you have come from
With your buried steps full of new roots?
You cannot leap up to look out,
Yet you do not sink,
But seem to grow, and the sound,
The oldest of sounds, is your breath
Sighing like acres.
If you stand as you are for long,

Green panic may finally give
Way to another sensation,
For when the embodying wind
Rises, the grasses begin to weave
A little, then all together,
Not bending enough for you
To see your way clear of the swaying,
But moving just the same,

And nothing prevents your bending
With them, helping their wave
Upon wave upon wave upon wave
By not opposing,
By willing your supple inclusion
Among fields without promise of harvest,
In their marvelous, spiritual walking
Everywhere, anywhere.

In the Mountain Tent

I am hearing the shape of the rain
Take the shape of the tent and believe it,
Laying down all around where I lie
A profound, unspeakable law.
I obey, and am free-falling slowly

Through the thought-out leaves of the wood
Into the minds of animals.
I am there in the shining of water
Like dark, like light, out of Heaven.

I am there like the dead, or the beast
Itself, which thinks of a poem—
Green, plausible, living, and holy—
And cannot speak, but hears,
Called forth from the waiting of things,

A vast, proper, reinforced crying
With the sifted, harmonious pause,
The sustained intake of all breath
Before the first word of the Bible.

At midnight water dawns
Upon the held skulls of the foxes
And weasels and tousled hares
On the eastern side of the mountain.
Their light is the image I make

As I wait as if recently killed,
Receptive, fragile, half-smiling,
My brow watermarked with the mark
On the wing of a moth

And the tent taking shape on my body
Like ill-fitting, Heavenly clothes.

From holes in the ground comes my voice
In the God-silenced tongue of the beasts.
"I shall rise from the dead," I am saying.